Shiva's Drum

Shiva's Drum

poems

BY STEPHEN CRAMER

UNIVERSITY OF ILLINOIS PRESS

Urbana and Chicago

1 2 3 4 5 C P 5 4 3 2 1

Library of Congress
Cataloging-in-Publication Data
Cramer, Stephen, 1975–
Shiva's drum : poems by Stephen Cramer.
p. cm. — (The national poetry series)
Includes bibliographical references.
ISBN 0-252-02959-3 (cl. : alk. paper)
ISBN 0-252-07204-9 (pbk. : alk. paper)
I. Title. II. Series.
PS3603.R365S55   2004
811'.6—dc22   2004007254

The National Poetry Series

The National Poetry Series was established in 1978 to ensure the publication of five poetry books annually through participating publishers. Publication is funded by the late James A. Michener, the Copernicus Society of America, Edward J. Piszek, the Lannan Foundation, the National Endowment for the Arts, and the Tiny Tiger Foundation.

2003 Competition Winners

Stephen Cramer of Astoria, New York
Shiva's Drum
Chosen by Grace Schulman; published by
University of Illinois Press

Andrew Feld of Eugene, Oregon
Citizen
Chosen by Ellen Bryant Voigt; published by
HarperCollins

Raymond McDaniel of Ann Arbor, Michigan
Entrance to Murder and After
Chosen by Anselm Hollo; published by
Coffee House Press

John Spaulding of Phoenix, Arizona
The White Train: Poems from Photographs
Chosen by Henry Taylor; published by
Louisiana State University Press

Mark Yakich of Oakland, California
Unrelated Individuals Forming a Group Waiting to Cross
Chosen by James Galvin; published by Penguin

Acknowledgments

Many thanks to the editors of the following publications in which these poems (some in earlier versions) first appeared:

Barrow Street:	"Abide with Me"
	"Out of Breath"
Brilliant Corners:	"Sunday"
Cimarron Review:	"Praise"
	"Sustained"
Confrontation:	"Off the Road"
Crab Orchard Review:	"Blanket"
Global City Review:	"What We Do"
High Plains Literary Review:	"Strange Drives"
The Journal:	"Calling"
Quarterly West:	"Desert Shadows"
	"Source"
	"The Whetstone"
South Dakota Review:	"For Brendan"
	"Honey"

I'm indebted and grateful to all my teachers, especially those whose influence and criticism helped most in shaping this book: Sascha Feinstein, G. W. Hawkes, and William Matthews. Thanks are also due to Scott Hightower; Denise Duhamel; and, of course, Grace Schulman, who in various and important ways provided much appreciated support along the way.

For my family,

for Joanna

In his upper right hand Shiva grips the hour-glass shaped drum
on which he beats the rhythms not only of music and sex
but also of time which ultimately extinguishes us. His cadence
encapsulates both creation and destruction in their endless
exchange and balance . . .

O teach me how to work and keep me kind. —Stanley Kunitz

Contents

For Brendan

I knew her first as the rhythm
     of her cane on the floor above—faint
lexicon of creaks and taps that let me
     invent her cramped apartment—the certain
television, the recliner, and withered

     ottoman she sidesteps to the kitchen.
But it's my neighbor's laugh that turns
     the ceiling's thick plaster to rice paper,
the same laugh that, outside, calls to her heels
     her scooter- and trike-propelled tribe

of neighborhood children, this extended family
     she's adopted because polio's kept her from kids
of her own. Outside the grocery she asks
     about my sister's second child. Two years
of agencies, I answer, and still paperwork'll

     keep him from her arms for weeks.
                        Texas,
a transitional family, and another imagined
     room—portable crib, plush mobile
dangling from the respirator, and a rainbowed
     circus whirls to his charted pulse.

The sweet anxieties of early parenthood.
     Two decades of marriage, it's 1975,
and my mother starts the new year
     with her *own* troubled pregnancy,
the early delivery that may not be early

enough. First hours on the other side of labor,
and a clergy absolves the failing child—
        prayers, fogging the surface of a plastic
womb, blur his gestures to vague curves.
        Then, once the child's prepared

for heaven, the doctors do their best
        to delay his trip, and he's wheeled away
to the last of four transfusions, the one
        that finally sustains him. Those anonymous
donors, their blood bagged and chilled

        to come alive again in me—I've never wondered
until today what their names might be,
        what community of fluids cruises my veins.
Little one, all this to tell you something simple:
        we're of one blood. The grocery's lights

fizzle and fade. My neighbor's dark skin deepens
        to twilight. I'm walking her home, a bag
in each hand, and she's describing
        the milk, eggs, flour, and the buttered
cornbread they'll become. When I pull out

        the photo of a child, curled, almost,
into a fist-sized ball, she props her cane
        against her door. *Ain't that something*, she says,
and laughs one of her two-syllabled laughs
        that truly means *ain't that something*.

Then she pauses, looks at the ground,
        and *honey*, she says, talking, now, almost
to herself, *if you knelt each time*
        a miracle passed your eyes,
you'd never get off your knees.

What We Do

A metallic detonation arcs
        over Broadway's gulf, and the aluminum
                contorts to contain the continuous
syncopation wrecked into its side—

        with two feet of pipe
                a man's beating a keg till it turns useless
for anything else but to carry
        his liquid rhythms. He's drumming

                a rim full of dents, angled
facets that pull to themselves
        all the sun they can bear before tossing
                a tremolo of light off the bricks behind.

Look around: whatever this sound is
        that ricochets the streets is contagious—
                less drums than a seasonal quickening
that everything's so busy keeping up with,

        new desire mixing up the thick torpor
                of the past months. At my feet,
two pigeons struggle over any spare
        piece of garbage to entice a female.

                They fumble in this patch of spilled popcorn,
gurgling and churring in figure eights,
        inflating the sheen of their necks
                over their turf. Even when she dodges

away, they just keep flashing iridescence
        for no one. Noontime, the drummer's checking
            the metal where he's reflected
in more than one place, tucking a stray

        curl behind his ear. But just so you don't
            forget whose block this is,
when a woman goes by
        he's sent demonic, like he knows

            this commotion's for keeps,
and he's thrown into a shimmy
        of the hips, which he rises out of
            just in time to fit the mechanical stumble

of a far-off jackhammer into his running
        cadence. These sounds the music *wants*
            to encompass, make its own,
so in the end, you can't tell if he's playing

        the drums or if they're playing him.
            Because when you're itching
to finish with your wrists
        the rumble that begins in your gut,

            this is what you do—you're ready
to bang on *anything* for love.
        You'll break your hands
            to get that rhythm out.

Sunday

In this heat wave everyone shifts
    self-consciously into church,
        pulling at their clothes

to ease the insistent chafe
    of rayon and polyester
        already dampening to stains.

But still a candle
    burns Pentecostal in the back,
        the allegory stronger than this need

to press hands and cheeks
    against the cool stone walls. On the curb,
        a street evangelist voices

Spanish verses from a Bible
    into a microphone, his shoulder
        heaving to a single burst

of *amens* inside, his voice projecting
    across the street to a woman mumbling
        about tomatoes shriveled in their skins

and the sterile sand of her lot.
    I'm walking by, fingering two tokens
        in my pocket, feeling the stretch

of everything for a drink—
        ginkgo roots pressing down
                from the sidewalk

to the blessing of cracked water pipes
        that maze beneath this city
                where everything searches

for that one way
        to edge past frustration,
                beneath the pavement blurring

in its own heat
        so what looks like a drying afghan
                from afar blooms into a drift

of peaches and sunflowers
        at a fruit stand, and the shapes
                of everything I think I know

shift in the haze
        until I step into the subway
                and voices give way

to the insinuation of a trumpet
        slipping phrases like hot silk
                through these tunnels

and I think of you
        who are farther away
                than next door, and how we have lit

a candle more than once
    to something we cannot see,
        something strange and sliding and uncontrollable

like this music
    winding through the porcelain
        of these crooked corridors

until it slips through a grate
    and fades between a siren and a horn.

Calling

How many swallows
lace the air between us
this dusk? A pair,

as I phone, skitter the air,
wreathe each other,
fall back to the same
stretch of wire.

Remember the eighteen
gulls on the bank—
how they took flight
for any stray wisp

of wind—even for a chipmunk
nosing the leaves—
then reassembled
and let us pass through,

balanced on eighteen legs
like we weren't even there?

Listen, you say
and hold the receiver
to the open window—

what I don't hear
is a hermit warbler
calling, trembling candles
on Arizona conifers.

I press, if possible, closer.

Hear it? you ask.
Then, to my silence,

I can hear you
nodding.

Honey

*Who's prepared to pay the price
for a trip to paradise?*

A deepening russet wash—flushed
memory of bees wedging through
bricks and floor beams—blooms
across my ceiling, all last summer
stores of hexagons overflowing
till their sap seeped through paint.
On the stereo, it's Billie, her late
years. I close my eyes to her creased
and swollen face, her voice hardened,
scraping lower notes as she loops
the cord on her fingers just to hold
something. Her lyrics—all facets of one
recurring plea to be held the way
her notes embrace the listener—gently,
close—and because she's not, the night
collapses and pales to cold sweat,
the back of the bus where she's holding
herself against a frosted window
lit with a new glow, each tilted
crystal shining from within. Amazing
how you can be so beat up
by something and still love it—
even scarred cats will clatter
past my shins toward the park
where dozens of strays roll over
onto unknown haunches, females

clawing their necks as they wail
for hours between bushes.
Billie, I've heard the stories—your last
dollars taped to your inner thigh
so no one could cheat you
your final due—and I never know,
when I hear you, how the life
that brought you to that
could create the balm, these nights,
that eases feeling back into
my fingertips, that lets me see again
on my ceiling not a damaged
paint job, but wreathes of honey
that unfold, for you, into one
last garland still burgeoning
into these dormant months.
All I know is this: no one's solace
is worth your life. So I want to keep
this picture of you blushing in amber
lights cut by smoke, lips curved
around a vowel you'll never sing.
Paused between breaths
just before you gave too much
to the song without the song
giving enough back, you're stilled
the way last year's honey
clung to my shingles, smothering
two bees in their own
sweetness, perfect wings bristling.

1963

A year before marriage, twelve
      before I'm born, and my mother misses
            the British invasion's repeated footage—
the first landing in the States when, the airstrip
      mobbed with sobbing girls, pimpled boys,
            the band was sure the President's jet

was inbound. Calcutta, a crowded street
      parts for a rickshaw, and my mother focuses,
            opens the aperture just in time to catch
a young girl, hands pressed together
      in greeting against a bicycle's blur. Mist of
            sandalwood. Gesture across the years.

The projector hums, and our chairs
      are rearranged like weather around
            the Ganges stirred by storm, the always-peopled
steps to the bank where water swells
      to meet a patchwork of laundry—draped
            sari diamonded by lit water behind, a turban

unraveled to its full drab length.
      Blocks away is the market
            where she returns a foot-high bronze
of Shiva to the street vendor
      for a pocket full of rupees. Too extravagant,
            she decides. But years later,

this is her trip's one regret—to have lost
            that hoop of stilled flame around the figure's
                        struck pose, one leg lifted in dance.
She can still see the skilled metalwork:
            in one hand, an hourglass-shaped drum
                        on which the other three, sculpting air,

can beat the palpitations that drive
            our blood, open our mouths to song
                        the way, on another continent, the stadium's
crowd would drown out all but their own
            adoration. Anthem of noise, so Ringo,
                        shaking his do behind his glittered kit,

beats waltz-time to "Can't Buy Me Love"
            and not even those close enough
                        to touch the towered speakers can tell.
Let's face it: this is their last
            chance to be young, to shake their untrimmed
                        locks across their eyes, before some are shipped

to an artilleried jungle, screaming not their favorite
            song but the glister of napalm across miles
                        of green. But this is not what I'm talking about,
only this photo of a man haloing the wall.
            Knee-deep in water, he stands the way
                        we come into this world, sky-clad,

gripping only a palm-sized drum. His torso
          and face smeared with ashes, for months
                    he's allied himself with silence, not even once
letting his fingers stir across its hollow. But because
          we hold closest to what's missing—a lost
                    statue, a drum's hide left unstruck—now

the camera's caught him rinsing gray
          from his body, shedding the quiet like a snake's
                    second skin. What else can you do
but align your blood with the rhythm
          that will take everything, even
                    your breath? Let's imagine this: swirls of ash

washing downstream all he didn't play, the hush
          growing so deep he could already hear
                    the next pulse seething inside it.

Blanket

Penn Station's cavernous staircase,
and two children whisper to the waists
of commuters—*please ma'am, God bless
you sir*—each time one drops coins
to the cardboard they hold.
But beneath the wilting trays,
their hands sift through pants—
deftly, even gracefully—easy enough
when people's sensations are lost
somewhere between missed cabs
and this backward syntax that sticks
in their mouths like sugar burnt
over peanuts on these corners.
Later, tallying cash and bruises,
the boys'll toss down a grate
the incidental keys to no place
they know. But now, when a nearby
woman approaches, cradling a baby,
they give each other looks. *Please,*
you say, *not her. Not her.*
But then, the timing just right,
the woman—I can't say this slowly
enough—she casts her baby
to the air—

                    and there are seconds
when the baby's suspended
with nowhere to land but pavement
before a stranger—what else to do?—
drops his bag to catch it. He's looking
for burns, expecting blood, when at once

the woman and two kids grab
what they can, which is
everything—bag, wallet, keys.

How long does it take him
to know this was a design, a ruse
repeated time and again to perfection?
This time two incidental cops disrupt
their practiced sequence so, trading
their sister, their daughter, for a slim
handful of spoils, the three turn into crowd,
and the man's left holding a child
at arm's length, lifting her to the sky
as though to bear witness that, yes,
here is a child, a breathing
prop, paused in a man's arms
before the landslide of years—before
her hands can grow streamlined
to pocket lining, before she can sell
herself beneath these tattered lights,
exchanging the cardboard for an orange
mesh tanktop with tears in all the right
places, her skin barely cupping
the curve of flesh where it swells
to deeper brown. But wait—none of this,
as yet, is so; something out there
wants to lift her from her own life. Look—
already someone opens a blanket
embroidered with a map to the air,
spreading India, Egypt, Peru, over her
shoulders arched against the siren.
And when they take her away,

that's the last anyone sees—
not a single finger or kneecap
of the girl, but only a blanket
that swaddles a lucky child
in the folds of a created world.

Three Little Birds, 130th Street

Midday's lull in Spanish Harlem,
and from a deli, for once, the familiar salsa
gives way to Marley's voice, wires unraveled
to let speakers reach the old folk's
card table of dominos. As the game

spreads between them, the buoyant
sweep of rhythm lifts through static
and I'm delivered to the back step of 56 Hope
Road, Kingston, the Tuff Gong rolling
spliffs, scribbling the occasional lyric

over the neck of his guitar. He tosses
the herb's seeds to the ground, to a few
lucky ground doves congregating to glean
the walk. Manhattan's no island
paradise, but still on the pavement

it's a fidgeting glint of wings—starlings
dropped from the eaves to strut
their own language of guttural trills
and metallic chirps, the raised angles
of their wings flagrant as the two lovers

embraced, here, in the corner's phone booth.
Lovers, I think, until her first muffled shriek,
and then he's not kissing but
choking her against the back, wedging
her neck to the glass with two

crossed thumbs. When he pulls away
for a second and she gets one good lungful
to cry out, he staggers up the street,
she retreats across traffic, and I'm in
her shadow unreeling a string of useless

questions—*You okay?* Closed eyes. *Did you
know him?* She did, and so we recross
the street to the deli's phone where still
the music absurdly carries on. *Every little thing
is gonna be all right,* Marley could claim

years before the assassination attempt
that failed, the cancer that didn't.
In the end, the chemo fell short,
and his precious locks unhinged
like heavy limbs, final as this scene

replaying in my head, the one that could end
with a kiss or hot sour breath
on the cheek, a stranded receiver,
and somehow the choice isn't mine.
What to make of it all then,

a melody pure and true? Sweetheart,
we're bruised into silence
or song. *This is my message to you.*

Two Tattoos

Fixed as his initials, T. H. C., the addict's parents
      etched one into his chest,
unlucky last name of Carter that let them fulfill
      what began as a barroom joke
and ended as a life, a son falling into the space
      between their laughter.
So eager, at three, to please—his cells already fired
      by a need he can't name,
he endured the needling in an hour-long chain
      of squeals before the small grinning
skull was shaped—vacant sockets that watched him,
      upside down, those nights when trying
to itch it off just made it swell. Child, let be
      the bones that stretch with your skin,
the years that expand them into an oblong
      smudge of a hollow face.
                                He could be the man
on the subway now, who grips the bar
      by his head, proud, in his tank top,
to exhibit this circle on his inner bicep—
      concentric blue lotus petals, spokes
that bend with the rise of a vein.
      And in the center, the only break
in symmetry, a diagonal slash
      of bruise-colored dye that, when he turns,
is held in relief against the moving dark,
      this dye which isn't dye
but stretched flesh, a burn, incorporated,
      enshrined. Imagine when he walks—
how the swelling must brush and brush

his chest, the friction now a reminder
not of what his graze with fire made him,
　　　but of what *he* has made of *it*—
how wounds, singular as any birthmark,
　　　can be tampered into indigo braids,
scarred into rainbow,
　　　ruinous in their beauty.

Desert Shadows

The name you use off the reservation
I forget. The more intimate one,
the one your parents use, recalled
the cloudy day your mother
spread her legs and grunted you
into this dry, dry air.
                        Desert sun
dissolves to showers minutes
after the horizon's first cloud.
You kept nodding the barkeep over,
lifting your finger for just one more
till your talk unfolded
to rags of clouds, to nights of slow
seduction, torture and—
                        then, the silence
which comes when too much
has been said, and ghosts smoke
in the air between us. You sit,
sip your Honey Amber, and count
the scars on your body—twenty-two,
no, -three—the burn between your fingers—
and when you're through you tell me
their tally is what you mean
when you say *where I'm from.*
You're not talking city or town
but the sky and blood that shaped you,
as rain shapes limestone into a perfect
cup. Recounting the story
of each contortion of skin
can spin you round and round,

make you slap the mama
you love, so you can't recall
twenty seconds ago before
you were filled with this rage
or desire. What could I do
in the face of stone eyes?
The moment I left, I vowed to forget.
Penetrating Shadow.
I walk into a dusky city,
repeating my name.

The Whetstone

Almost metallic, almost guttural—
      at times the sound's so plaintive,
it could just about pass for human—
      this deep, grated hum at corridor's end,
42nd Street. I'm drawn less by the music

      itself than by memory's blind pull,
the twanged vibrato half-triggering—what?—
      already the moment's gone, and I'm left
with the shift and commingling of the crowd.
      Then, there he is—a man's dragging a bow

across the smooth edge of a three-foot
      hand saw—unlikely vehicle—his free hand
gliding then grappling, bending the metal
      to impossible notes the workshop
never dreamed of. Curve on top of

      curve—his creening neck mirrors the hard
arc of steel as it curls to follow
      a cascaded run of notes showered
from the tape deck beside him.
      His shuddering forearm seismic,

his wrist all nuance, he lets vibration
      polish rust to a silver burn, the metal
warped out of utility just to prove
      that anything—the busted tools
marooned in basement shadows—

can be contorted into song. Memory's
blind pull, then I close my eyes and
        I'm there in the dank cellar of the house
my grandfather built—strung roots
        dangling, drill bits hung in diminishing rows—

all he left behind. Back from the chapel's
        service, I palmed his cross-hatched
whetstone, rubbing it to feel
        the years, hearing, almost,
the insistent whistle of his bait-knives

        and shears, the sinuous vocabulary
of scraping noises—rasp, grind,
        sputter—elevated, like this saw's
fizzled solo, to music. I'll retain
        from his life no lofty moment—

not the words of one intimate
        exchange—but a humble sense
of accuracy. If he were here
        now, he might not be able to articulate
all the facets of loss, but he'd tell me

        how many tiles trimmed this wall
to resonance, while all I try to say
        grinds to dust, coiled shavings.
After all our efforts, what lasts
        besides the endless shaping

toward precision? Any memorial's
      inadequate, double sided
as this man's blade still shimmying
      before me—one edge can slice you
while the other keeps singing.

Abide with Me

If she can't trace the cloudy
    synapses that lead to her daughter's
        name, still my mother's mother
can accompany Monk's ensemble,

her throat trembling the high notes
    over the last state line before home—
        fast falls the eventide. She no longer
owns the strength to produce

all the sounds the spirit contains, songs
    from her other life when the Church
        lifted her even from the sudden fall
down the garden path that left her leg

useless. Home, the stale odor
    of a weeklong absence mixes
        with a smell we can't name until we find
the sink spattered with white

and the glass birds fractured,
    sticky with real, matted feathers.
        Then it's just a matter of finding
the catbird in the corner

who must've hurled himself
    again and again toward nothing,
        wounding these trinkets
until he owned their stone wings.

This morning, she wipes the pane
        smudgeless then rocks her chair further
                and further from this palmful of life
that couldn't get out the way you hope

you will. Fast falls. What will stay with you
        as these lyrics have remained with her,
                what words to nudge you through
until you're riding the last even tide,

rocking toward a sheen of clouds
        where the last thing you see is your own
                face before you pass through to light
or shatter with the trying?

Praise

If there is anything worthy of praise, think about these things.

In the aftershock of bells
         even more ruined plaster
    sifts down to chiseled
saints hooded in sheets,

    adding to the list of things
I want to show you—

flakes of concrete falling like glitter
        in early light. When you're around,
    you charge everything I see.
But without you, even this slow

    drift of Sunday pastel
as the congregation gathers outside

seems laced with melancholy,
        until they start to sing
    and wave their hymnals,
shaking hand-painted maracas

as they sway on the tide of glory
    that catches down the block—

a man blows his horn across
        the street, edging so close to failure
    as if to tiptoe the brink
before swinging back to chorus

that I want to get lost
in the thin air between sixteenth

notes where ache's been purified
            in clouded brass and blown
        as praise. On these streets where
each corner tests the miracle

        we keep *not* getting hit,
the only way to get by

is to let music caress
            the unguided ruin of it all—
        the crowd outside singing so loud and fluid
that even in the park I step in time

        to *we are walking in the light*
until my shirt is damp with sweat

and I want to praise
            this pulse of the glands
        that taints each breath
with the rhythm of desire

        so even plaid double Dutch
blends with the syncopated clicks

of a lame dog's claws
            as he tracks fleeing shadows
        of sticks. I'm overwhelmed again
like the time we parted

           roadside grasses to uncover
wildflowers, astounded by names

as much as the way stamens
                dusted our palms with pollen
           as we bent to foxglove beardtongue,
trailing arbutus, rough

           vines of cinquefoil.
That summer, the rip in your jeans,

the ink stains on your stockings
                made me forget my name.
           Sunlight, now, through spires.
Going home with the taste

           of honey so sweet it numbs
the side of my tongue.

Baby, in the way you turned
                to push further through hemlocks,
           in the way light bent
to touch the soft

           curve of your clavicle,
I've found something

I would kneel to
                again and again.

Late Hours
(Sonnets for Stanley Kunitz)

I

The whole day you changed just one word.
       Eyes closed over a typewriter,
             testing sounds on the air, you read

in a swell of undulating whispers,
       one shoulder rhythmically heaving. June,
             the first year out on the sun-drenched Cape,

you spread seaweed on the barren dune
       of your yard with a wooden rake.
             Mounds of peat moss, rotting compost

and saplings still wrapped in burlap
       scattered the terraced slope. Exhausted
             at night, with fingers crusted in sap

and caked soil streaked on your forehead,
       you imagined morning glories in bed.

II

This morning, as the flower bed,
     showered with veronica and anemones,
          tilts like gulls angled in wind overhead,

your hands rustle among honey bees
     that nudge the coral bells and sway
          in the brine-filled air. Snakes on spruce bark

coil where you kneel to pinch decayed
     and wilted petals, cutting back
          clumped disease like a crossed-out line,

making way for a flash of cardinal flower among
     the hedgerow in this poem you refine
          with tool-calloused fingers each spring.

You weed leaning stalks of bergamot,
     torn and spotted leaves nodding in pooled light.

III

You're onstage, awash in the spotlight,
        rubbing the back of your ear with two fingers,
            squinting into memory. Slight

pause between syllables as you conjure
        the scene—a dusty road in Quinnapoxet,
            evenings fishing at the reservoir—

and you shuffle your hand in your pocket,
        lean into the mic with a hunched shoulder
            as if with a crooked stance

you could press from your body words
        to punctuate the air and pulse
            against the high walls of the theater,

your voice blooming outward to each
        person breathing quiet in his seat.

IV

When you leaned forward in the seat
        driving back to the city that night,
                you described and shaped in air the plants heated

in a blush of hung citron lights
        all those winters in your apartment
                and how you couldn't wait to get out

in spring to auger your hands through loose dirt.
        When you asked my favorite poets
                ("present company excepted")

I stumbled, tried to make you understand
        you were the one I'd read and reread,
                the one I'd always imagined

easily tapping out perfect lines each day,
        each year. So, tell me now, what could I say?

V

Now, given time, I *know* what I'd say:
  I understand more fully the effort
    of drafts, the mulch of those thrown away.

I'd tell you I've always pictured
  that old poets actually sink
    into spaces between their words. So now, these late

hours, I imagine your creased skin
  under a Greek fisherman's hat,
    and the wild, white hair beneath. Pen in hand

after staying up all night, you wait
  for the rapture to "break on your mind."
    Lines spill on paper, and as you shape

and reshape them, you fade deeper into work,
  gradually changing to a word.

Source

You could begin with my second
day, how the doctors withdrew
and the clergy stepped up
to render last rites. I made it
through the unknown mutiny
of blood with only my hearing
lost. It's because I was deaf
for my first few months
that now I'm kindled by song,
and I listen for riffs to
itch my fingers awake. The click
and rasp of high heels
is a lubricant to blues. In this
city of facade and fever,
I'm shanghaied to a dream,
some species of luck tugging
the prettiest girl in the street
to my arms. I'm always cornered
by love at 2 A.M. I don't know
what good fortune kept me
here, what awaits, only
that I'm located somewhere
between a come-cry
and dust, and I can only tell
how close I am to the first.
Remember this—absolved
in my first hours, I got free reign
for everything I'm gonna get
all wrong. I can feel your

breath like I can feel the surge
of roots beneath these stones
because I'm a dangerous mix
of beauty marks and scars.

Stained-Glass Maker

Whole days he spends
      searching out materials—ambers
and greens locked in bottles,
      lucky burgundy of a broken taillight—

          each piece charged with tangled
fissures that pull intensity
      to themselves, blues rupturing

to deeper blue. Other mornings,
      like this one, he drops
to the pavement his finds—a crash
      the neighbors have had to relearn

          as one of creation. Then he bends
as though divining futures
      in what looks like a fauvist

cloud fringed with lavender,
      edged with unusable dust,
tinted splinters of shining.
      I try to hold in speech

          the shapes—abrupt wedges of salmon,
trapezoidal chips glinting
      against each other—but how to seize

in words this amorphous spread of glitter
      that catches your breath in whirls
of sheen rich and varied as music
      ripped apart and pieced back together?

Memory holds to me a gnarled
shaft, the length of a javelin,
     crumbling in museum fluorescents—

lightning fossilized where it tunneled
     through a beach, scorching
sand to glass. I thought it impossible
     to sleeve the path of light,

          but here was this continuous record
of the dazzling. In the same way,
     I try to catch the luminous patterns,

though I know I'll be left not
     with the mythical flash of inspiration
but a fractured column, paled
     in description, a reference for where light

          once was, though the last of it
was spent on the thrill of the making,
     the gradual solidification of detail,

mysterious as any birth. By twilight,
     the glass is shaped to souls striding
on waves of color, speaking light
     over a crackling city of gold—

          all held by seams of solder
so thick it's the brokenness,
     if anything, that makes it worthy

of attention—his windows hold back
	as much as they let through.
On the corner, now, his hunched profile
	is the absence of sky. That's how it is

		when you glean the curbs, when you
search out shards of light in this slow
	work of piecing things together.

Sustained

A concert in the cathedral
and I can't help but describe
the strange and sudden architecture

      of sound. Architecture, I say,
      but mean not stone, only the air

the stone contains, which fills now,
as bass swells in the vaulting
then recoils, folding back into itself

      as a wave. Then, a voice—this woman
      grasping at invisible strands before her,

climbing a delicate rope that isn't there,
hand over hand until she coaxes the peak
of the scale, then cascades in a tumble

      of notes, so she herself seems to fall,
      crumpling like a discarded shirt

on the stage. These real, sweat-streaked
tears on her cheeks leave behind
all her artifice—the diamond-studded

      glow of dangled earrings that swing
      when she does but don't stop

when she stills, just keep brushing
her neck, afterthought made visible,
the way her lyrics spread and resound

      even as she takes a breath—
      not echo exactly, but a sustaining,

as though the music were remembering
itself in the air above us. I'm taken
to the heavy-lidded morning you left,

      when I returned alone from the station.
      A man was balancing his way

through subway cars, wailing harmonica
so loud we could only feel, not hear,
the rumble beneath us. His free hand

      shook as though stuttering,
      intricately, in sign language.

After your bus left I held you
like the last note he played—only
in my mind. Home, I went to call you,

      to leave a message, a small light
      blinking in your empty apartment,

saying, *I'm here.* I don't know
what I meant to say, something vague
about appreciation. But I paused—

the receiver was washed
with your fragrance, magnolia,

and it spread onto my skin.
You know what they say—
how an object of desire

makes *you* more beautiful.
Tonight, the woman's so fastened

to her words that each new lyric
makes her shine—a single blue spot
sapphires her black skin, and her gown

darkens to sweat as lights bloom
across its lace. Each new verse

sends me wheeling toward a story—
how among the Slavs, women
would kneel to the footprint

of a loved one, would dig it up
and pot it, would plant a single seed,

a perennial, in its center
to ensure long love. Hungering
for the other, they're decked out

in the most delicate petals.
I imagine people crouching

to wet earth after rain. The work
of the music that is sweat
and love. And isn't that how

      we should begin, with this sustained
      note held like a breath,

the scent of each other
lingering on our cheeks all day?

In the Cathedral, Before the Sky

What heaven we had we made.
  —Lynda Hull

In a marble niche, techniques you wouldn't expect
to find here—the canvas stocked
not with dainty jots to match the background glow

of stained glass but with whole slabs of color
as though this sudden tumult of amber
nimbus had been applied with spoons.

Even the frame's gilded in braids
of gold and silver with periodic crescendos
of rosettes as if to represent heaven spilling

through, the borders crammed with excess.
But it's all so lavish I can't help feeling
the man prostrate here kneels not to the prospect

of a land beyond, swathed in unknowable light,
but to the handiwork, the sweat and weeks spent
driving the shapes to precision. If we can only

imagine heaven in our own terms, it'll always
be a fusion of luxuries gathered from here.
Who ever envisioned for themselves a setting

without what they love most? When *we* disappear,
Love, let it be into this—*all* the disjointed
matter of the land, not just the alluring,

but the plain ore before it's extracted, melted,
pounded to that thin stretch of gleaming.
Let it be into the swirls of these paints

I can't even look at without feeling the ground
that birthed them—dark clay crushed
with elderberry, huge spaces of cadmium

that unfold into wisps of sky, all barely able
to contain a bird that soars not heaven
but in this very earth—where else could the clouds

look so troubled and dazzling?

Strange Drives

We blame the first low planet,
tilted in some weird phase,
or the swoop of a flycatcher—
anything but my family.

Birdwatchers and stargazers
make the worst drivers.
But it's hardly our fault: sparrows,
buntings, the sun-doused hawk

hypnotize our glance
as we swivel in rhythm
and glance rhythmically
left, road, right, road.

Concerned passengers know
how interesting highways look
and rigidly stare them down,
use mind power to bend the car

to soft curves, a tricky gift
that doesn't always work.
Recently, my family's admitted
our hobbies are best enjoyed

outside. We've made rules—
even a quick jab, finger
to window, is taboo. Now,
when warblers send others

avidly slanting toward weedy
warning tracks, we shake our heads
and swear mild curses
of those who understand.

Rehearsal

Not the best we've heard,
    but the band's good enough, at times,
to make you keep saying, *feel that,*
        you feel that? like the music
            was the silk
                        and sequined
jacket of the drummer
    I could walk up to and stroke
till my hands bled with the knowing.
        But what I feel is the bass line
            flushed
                    through your fingers
as the horn fractures to indigo
    combinations, discovering how to match
the night's urgent tug into wilderness,
        and your fingers fist
            when the snare
                        urges him
so deep into melody
    that the bridge he blows is the air
on our backs, the lamp outside
        whirling light. Another kiss
            and I taste the lime
                        your lips stole
from the rim of my beer, the way
        the right song can rephrase
your insides into sound
        so your own unimaginable taste
            is redelivered
                    to your tongue.

It doesn't matter if the pianist
        lags, if he doesn't quite leap
to chorus in time, because this is why
        they're at it night after night
                in any dive
                        that'll house them.
We pull together as though we aimed
        to arrive, impossibly, on the other side
of each other, a need we'll spend
        all night gratefully failing at,
                a need that'll steal us
                        from our seats
long before the rings on these napkins dry,
        as the last sizzle of a high hat
ushers us to the street,
        to the next perfect shortcoming
                and the next.

Out of Breath

Thank you for the way
the sun dismantled the clouds
or for the subterranean rumblings
of the subway, whichever paused me
long enough for the clay pot
to crash the pavement two strides
ahead. Instead of broken bones
I only ended up in the middle
of an awkward shuffle through shards
and spattered dirt that must've looked
like a dance with myself, an out-of-kilter
tiptoe around scattered petals.

I don't know what made my feet
circle the block to reenter the scene,
what made my hands gather the pile
of roots or press a severed stem into soil
in a curious impulse to care
for this that could've killed me. What
ancient rite moved my fingers?
In dim hind memory, a clan
huddled a carcass picked clean,
till one whittled a bone hollow
so the marrow gave way
to a stream of air, a channel
where he could breathe
strings of notes—not for the sound
but to prove death could be made
into something boundless,
something only air can hold.

I knelt to the remains
naturally as those wrists bent
to hollow springbok horn,
coaxing the animal's last whinny
into a bass tone that rumbles
the bones, a bellowed decibel
to throw your feet into dance
till you, too, are out of breath.

How I left on the sidewalk
a shallow garden of upright stems.
What else do you do
when you're given this
sustaining gift, when flowers
are falling from the sky?

Off the Road

Traveler, there is no road.
You make the road as you walk.
                    —Antonio Machado

Every road leads somewhere.
Except this one.
Outside the truck, you know
just how far your breath ghosts
from the next traffic light,
pulsing amber to empty streets.

Ridges of sand, a dim
memory of a sneaker sole,
keep you lost.
If you're on a path,
my feet say,
you're on the wrong one.

I'm learning to track
the descending spiral
of a canyon wren's love cry.
I bite my lip,
and its music is the blood
on my tongue.

This is the language
of my glands.
Only the smallest hairs

on the back of my neck
know what I mean
to say next.

Notes

"What We Do" is for Mike B.

"Calling" is for Adrea.

"Honey": this poem's epigraph is lifted from Cole Porter's song "Love for Sale."

"Two Tattoos": T. H. C. stands for tetrahydrocannabinol, the active ingredient in marijuana.

"Praise": this epigraph is taken from Philippians 4:8.

"Late Hours" is a crown of sonnets. Sort of. Though the final line of each sonnet is mirrored in the first line of the next, traditionally this form consists of seven to fourteen pieces.

Illinois Poetry Series
Laurence Lieberman, Editor

National Poetry Series

Eroding Witness
Nathaniel Mackey (1985)
Selected by Michael S. Harper

Palladium
Alice Fulton (1986)
Selected by Mark Strand

Cities in Motion
Sylvia Moss (1987)
Selected by Derek Walcott

The Hand of God and a Few
Bright Flowers
William Olsen (1988)
Selected by David Wagoner

The Great Bird of Love
Paul Zimmer (1989)
Selected by William Stafford

Stubborn
Roland Flint (1990)
Selected by Dave Smith

The Surface
Laura Mullen (1991)
Selected by C. K. Williams

The Dig
Lynn Emanuel (1992)
Selected by Gerald Stern

My Alexandria
Mark Doty (1993)
Selected by Philip Levine

The High Road to Taos
Martin Edmunds (1994)
Selected by Donald Hall

Theater of Animals
Samn Stockwell (1995)
Selected by Louise Glück

The Broken World
Marcus Cafagña (1996)
Selected by Yusef Komunyakaa

Nine Skies
A. V. Christie (1997)
Selected by Sandra McPherson

Lost Wax
Heather Ramsdell (1998)
Selected by James Tate

So Often the Pitcher Goes to
Water until It Breaks
Rigoberto González (1999)
Selected by Ai

Renunciation
Corey Marks (2000)
Selected by Philip Levine

Manderley
Rebecca Wolff (2001)
Selected by Robert Pinsky

Theory of Devolution
David Groff (2002)
Selected by Mark Doty

Rhythm and Booze
Julie Kane (2003)
Selected by Maxine Kumin

Shiva's Drum
Stephen Cramer (2004)
Selected by Grace Schulman

Other Poetry Volumes

Local Men and Domains
James Whitehead (1987)

Her Soul beneath the Bone:
Women's Poetry on Breast Cancer
Edited by Leatrice Lifshitz (1988)

Days from a Dream Almanac
Dennis Tedlock (1990)

Working Classics: Poems on
Industrial Life
Edited by Peter Oresick and Nicholas Coles
(1990)

Hummers, Knucklers, and
Slow Curves: Contemporary
Baseball Poems
Edited by Don Johnson (1991)

The Double Reckoning of
Christopher Columbus
Barbara Helfgott Hyett (1992)

Selected Poems
Jean Garrigue (1992)

New and Selected Poems, 1962-92
Laurence Lieberman (1993)

The Dig and Hotel Fiesta
Lynn Emanuel (1994)

For a Living: The Poetry of Work
Edited by Nicholas Coles and Peter Oresick
(1995)

The Tracks We Leave:
Poems on Endangered Wildlife
of North America
Barbara Helfgott Hyett (1996)

Peasants Wake for Fellini's
Casanova and Other Poems
Andrea Zanzotto; edited and translated by
John P. Welle and Ruth Feldman; drawings
by Federico Fellini and Augusto Murer
(1997)

Moon in a Mason Jar and What
My Father Believed
Robert Wrigley (1997)

The Wild Card: Selected Poems,
Early and Late
Karl Shapiro; edited by Stanley Kunitz and
David Ignatow (1998)

Turtle, Swan and Bethlehem in
Broad Daylight
Mark Doty (2000)

Illinois Voices: An Anthology of
Twentieth-Century Poetry
Edited by Kevin Stein and G. E. Murray
(2001)

On a Wing of the Sun
Jim Barnes (3-volume reissue, 2001)

Poems
William Carlos Williams; introduction by
Virginia M. Wright-Peterson (2002)

Creole Echoes:
The Francophone Poetry of
Nineteenth-Century Louisiana
Translated by Norman R. Shapiro;
introduction and notes by M. Lynn Weiss
(2003)

Poetry from *Sojourner:*
A Feminist Anthology
Edited by Ruth Lepson with Lynne
Yamaguchi; introduction by Mary
Loeffelholz (2004)

Asian American Poetry:
The Next Generation
Edited by Victoria M. Chang;
foreword by Marilyn Chin (2004)

The University of Illinois Press
is a founding member of the
Association of American University Presses.

————————————————————

The text typeface is Hoefler Type Foundry Requiem,
which is derived from a set of inscriptional capitals
appearing in Ludovico Vicentino degli Arrighi's
1523 writing manual, *Il Modo de Temperare le Penne.*

The display type is Will-Harris House's Tagliente,
based on the copybooks of a renowned
16th-century Italian writing master.

Designed and typeset by Michael J. Balzano

Manufactured by Thomson-Shore, Inc.

UNIVERSITY OF ILLINOIS PRESS
1325 South Oak Street   Champaign, IL 61820-6903
www.press.uillinois.edu